Aromatherapy: the natural path to your pet's well-being

By Gonzalo Estrada

AROMATHERAPY, THE NATURAL PATH TO YOUR PET´S WELL BEING

First edition. March 12, 2024.

Copyright © 2024 Gonzalo Estrada.

ISBN: 979-8224212972

Written by Gonzalo Estrada.

Table of Contents

Contents 1

Chapter 1: Introduction to Aromatherapy for Pets 2

Chapter 2: The Basic Principles of Aromatherapy 6

Chapter 3: Importance of Safety in Aromatherapy for Pets 10

Chapter 4: How to Choose the Right Essential Oils for Your Pet. 14

Chapter 5: Aromatherapy for Pet Stress and Anxiety 18

Chapter 6: Benefits of Aromatherapy in Caring for Your Pet's Skin 22

Chapter 7: Aromatherapy to ease digestive distress in pets 26

Chapter 8: Aromatherapy for your pet's respiratory well-being 30

Chapter 9: Aromatherapy for Pain and Inflammation Relief in Pets 34

Chapter 10: Aromatherapy for Emotional Support for Pets 38

Chapter 11: Aromatherapy for flea and tick management in pets. 42

Chapter 12: Aromatherapy for the care of your pet's coat 46

Chapter 13: Aromatherapy for the Relief of Separation Anxiety in Pets 49

Chapter 14: Aromatherapy for Aging in Pets 53

Chapter 15: Aromatherapy for Pet Training and Socialization 57

Chapter 16: Aromatherapy for energy balance in pets 61

Chapter 17: Aromatherapy for Pet Disease Prevention 65

Chapter 18: Aromatherapy for Strengthening Pet Immune Systems 69

Chapter 19: Aromatherapy as an Adjunct to Veterinary Medicine 73

Chapter 20: Aromatherapy Recipes for Caring for Your Pet 77

Contents

Chapter 1: Introduction to Aromatherapy for Pets

Chapter 2: The Basic Principles of Aromatherapy

Chapter 3: Importance of Safety in Aromatherapy for Pets

Chapter 4: How to Choose the Right Essential Oils for Your Pet

Chapter 5: Aromatherapy for Pet Stress and Anxiety

Chapter 6: Benefits of Aromatherapy in Caring for Your Pet's Skin

Chapter 7: Aromatherapy to ease digestive distress in pets

Chapter 8: Aromatherapy for your pet's respiratory well-being

Chapter 9: Aromatherapy for Pain and Inflammation Relief in Pets

Chapter 10: Aromatherapy for Emotional Support for Pets

Chapter 11: Aromatherapy for flea and tick management in pets

Chapter 12: Aromatherapy for the care of your pet's coat

Chapter 13: Aromatherapy for the Relief of Separation Anxiety in Pets

Chapter 14: Aromatherapy for Aging in Pets

Chapter 15: Aromatherapy for Pet Training and Socialization

Chapter 16: Aromatherapy for energy balance in pets

Chapter 17: Aromatherapy for the Prevention of Diseases in Pets

Chapter 18: Aromatherapy for Strengthening Pet Immune Systems

Chapter 19: Aromatherapy as an Adjunct to Veterinary Medicine

Chapter 20: Aromatherapy Recipes for Caring for Your Pet

Chapter 1: Introduction to Aromatherapy for Pets

Learn what aromatherapy is and how it can benefit your pet's overall well-being.

Have you ever wondered how you can improve your pet's quality of life in a natural and harmonious way? The answer can be found in aromatherapy, a practice that uses essential oils to promote health and well-being in our furry companions. In this first chapter, you'll dive into the fascinating world of aromatherapy to discover how it can benefit your pet's overall well-being.

Aromatherapy is an ancient discipline that originated in ancient Egypt and has been used for centuries in various cultures. It consists of the therapeutic use of essential oils, highly concentrated substances extracted from plants, flowers, fruits and herbs. These oils have natural properties that can have positive effects on people's bodies, minds and spirits, and the same goes for our beloved pets.

The application of aromatherapy to animals has become an increasingly popular alternative. Properly used essential oils can contribute to the emotional, physical and mental balance of our furry friends. However, it's important to note that not all essential oils are safe for pets, as their organisms have significant differences from ours.

Before starting to introduce aromatherapy into your pet's life, it's crucial to consider some basic considerations. First, make sure that the essential oils you use are of high quality and one hundred percent pure.

Avoid those that contain chemicals or additives, as they could be harmful to your pet.

In addition, the amount and frequency of use are fundamental aspects to consider. Remember that pets are more sensitive than humans, so very dilute doses must be used. It is always recommended to consult a veterinarian or professional specializing in aromatherapy for personalized guidance depending on the species and the individual needs of your pet.

Aromatherapy for pets can encompass a wide range of benefits for their overall well-being. Some of the aspects where it can positively impact include managing stress and anxiety, strengthening the immune system, improving sleep quality, and reducing skin and digestive problems.

Essential oils can be used in different ways and applied appropriately depending on the animal species. For example, for dogs and cats, you can opt for diffusion in the environment or topical application in the form of gentle massages in specific areas. It's critical to look at your pet's individual reactions and preferences, as everyone can respond differently to essential oils.

As you enter the world of aromatherapy for pets, you'll be amazed at the positive results you can get. However, remember that the safety and well-being of your pet should always be the priority. That's why, in the second part of this chapter, we'll explore in detail the most recommended essential oils, as well as the additional precautions you should consider when using them.

Get ready to discover how aromatherapy can transform your pet's well-being and bring their quality of life to unsuspected levels! Don't miss the second part of this chapter, where we'll delve into the secrets of essential oils and how to apply them safely and effectively. Your pet will thank you!

In this second part of our introductory chapter to aromatherapy for pets, we'll explore in depth the most recommended essential oils and the additional precautions you should consider when using them.

As we enter the world of essential oils, it's important to note that not all of them are safe for our pets. Some oils can be toxic or irritating to them, so it's critical to research and carefully choose those that are safe and beneficial.

One of the most popular and safe essential oils for pets is lavender oil. Not only does this oil have a pleasant scent, it is also known for its relaxing and soothing properties. You can use it to help your pet combat stress, anxiety and insomnia. In addition, lavender oil also has antiparasitic properties, so it can help repel fleas and ticks naturally.

Another safe and beneficial essential oil is chamomile oil. This oil is known for its anti-inflammatory and soothing properties, so it can help relieve muscle and joint pain in your pet. It is also effective in reducing skin irritation and relieving insect bites.

Tangerine essential oil is another pet favorite. This oil has a sweet, citrusy scent that can help calm anxiety and stress. Plus, it's thought to boost your pet's appetite, which is especially helpful if you have a dog or cat with little interest in food.

If you're looking for an essential oil to promote the health of your pet's immune system, tea tree essential oil can be an excellent choice. This oil is known for its antiviral, antifungal and antibacterial properties. You can use it to help your pet fight infections and strengthen their immune system.

Of course, it's crucial to remember that every pet is unique and can have individual reactions to essential oils. Therefore, it is always recommended to perform a sensitivity test before using any new oil. You can dilute a small amount of the oil in a carrier oil, such as coconut oil or almond oil, and apply it to a small area of your pet's skin. Watch for any reactions or signs of discomfort over the next few hours and adjust the dosage or type of oil as needed.

In addition, it is important to note that pets have a much more developed sense of smell than ours, so aromas can be more intense and can affect them differently. Always be sure to dilute essential oils and use very dilute doses to avoid any risk of irritation or discomfort.

Remember, your pet's safety and well-being should always be your priority. It is always recommended to consult a veterinarian or professional specializing in aromatherapy for personalized guidance depending on the species and the individual needs of your pet.

In short, aromatherapy for pets can be a powerful tool to promote their overall well-being. Essential oils can be used safely and effectively to help calm stress and anxiety, strengthen the immune system, improve sleep quality, and treat skin and digestive problems.

With the right knowledge and the necessary precautions, aromatherapy can transform your pet's well-being and bring their quality of life to unsuspected levels. So don't hesitate to explore this fascinating world of aromatherapy and discover how you can improve the life of your faithful companion in a natural and harmonious way.

Your pet will thank you!

Chapter 2: The Basic Principles of Aromatherapy

Learn the basics of aromatherapy adapted to the specific needs of pets.

Aromatherapy has been widely recognized for its therapeutic benefits in humans, but did you know that it can also be beneficial for your beloved pets? Yes, you read that right. Aromatherapy can be a natural and effective way to promote well-being in your four-legged companions.

Before diving into the wonderful experience of aromatherapy for pets, it's critical to understand the basic principles of how it works and how to safely adapt it for use in different species.

First of all, we must understand that essential oils are the pure and concentrated essence of plants and flowers. These essences have unique properties that can positively affect the mind, body and spirit of our pets. However, not all essences are safe for use in animals, as their olfactory and metabolic systems are different from ours.

Safety is paramount when using aromatherapy on pets. It is always advisable to consult a veterinarian or a professional trained in animal aromatherapy before starting any treatment. They will be able to guide and advise on safe essential oils and appropriate forms of application.

When adapting aromatherapy for use in pets, it's essential to remember that animals are much more sensitive to odors than we are. What may be pleasant and relaxing for us can be overwhelming or even irritating for them. Therefore, we must always dilute essential oils with a carrier or base oil before application.

There are several ways in which we can use aromatherapy with our pets. A common way is through the diffusion of essential oils into the environment. Not only will this help create a calm and relaxing environment for your pet, it can also benefit their mood and overall well-being.

Another way to apply aromatherapy to pets is by applying it topically. However, we must be extremely cautious when doing so, as some oils can irritate your skin or cause allergic reactions. It's essential to properly dilute oils and perform a sensitivity test on a small area of your skin before using them more widely.

In addition to diffusion and topical application, special blends can also be created for use in therapeutic massages. A gentle massage with the right essential oils will not only provide relaxation and stress relief to your pet, but it will also strengthen the bond between you and your pet.

Importantly, each animal species is unique and may respond differently to essential oils. While some oils may be beneficial for dogs, they may not be suitable for cats or rabbits. Therefore, it is essential to do your research before using any essential oil on your pet.

Thus, we have begun to enter the interesting world of aromatherapy adapted to the needs of our beloved pets. As we move through this chapter, we'll explore the different essential oils that can benefit your life partners, as well as additional precautions and tips to ensure their well-being and safety.

Remember, aromatherapy can be a wonderful tool for the well-being of your pets, but you always need to seek professional guidance and be aware of the individuality of each animal. Get ready to discover more about the benefits of aromatherapy in the second half of this chapter! The first half of this chapter has given us an overview of the basic principles of aromatherapy adapted to the needs of our pets. We have learned about the importance of safety when using essential oils, proper dilution, different forms of application and the individuality of each animal species. Now, it's time to dive deeper into the benefits and precautions associated with some specific essential oils and explore different ways to incorporate aromatherapy into the lives of our beloved pets.

Let's start by talking about some popular essential oils that can be beneficial to our pets. One of the most common oils used in aromatherapy for pets is lavender oil. This oil is known for its relaxing and calming properties. It can help relieve stress, anxiety and promote healthy sleep in our pets. However, it's important to remember that every pet is unique and may respond differently to essential oils, so we should always watch for any signs of discomfort or irritation.

Another essential oil that can be beneficial for our pets is chamomile oil. Known for its anti-inflammatory and soothing properties, it can be useful in relieving itching, inflammation and irritations on the skin of our pets. Because of its mild properties, chamomile oil is often recommended for cats and rabbits, which are known to be species more sensitive to essential oils.

In addition to these, there are many other essential oils that can be beneficial to our pets, such as tea tree oil, rosemary oil and lemongrass oil. Each of these oils has unique properties and can be used for different purposes, such as promoting skin and coat health, relieving muscle and joint pain, or even repelling insects.

However, it's important to remember that aromatherapy is not a substitute for proper veterinary care. It's always advisable to consult a veterinarian before using any essential oil on your pet, especially if they have a pre-existing medical condition or are taking other medications. A veterinarian will be able to provide you with specific guidance on which essential oil is safe and recommended for your particular pet.

In addition to the right choice of essential oils, it is also essential to be aware of additional precautions and advice to ensure the safety and well-being of our pets. Remember that pets, especially dogs, can be curious and can lick or ingest any substance that is applied to them. For this reason, it's important to ensure that essential oil blends are not toxic or harmful if ingested. Always use quality essential oils that are pure and safe for use on pets.

In addition, it is essential to keep essential oils out of reach of our pets. Storing them in a safe place out of reach will ensure their safety. It's also important to consider the individual sensitivity of our pets. Some pets may have sensitivities to certain essential oils, so we should always watch for any changes in their behavior or signs of discomfort after exposure to the oils.

In short, aromatherapy adapted to the needs of our pets can be a wonderful tool to promote their well-being and happiness. As we continue to explore more about this fascinating topic, it's important to remember the importance of safety, proper dilution, careful choice of essential oils, and consultation with a veterinarian. Aromatherapy can be an enriching experience for both our pets and us, as long as it's done responsibly.

With this, we conclude the second half of this chapter on the basic principles of aromatherapy adapted to the needs of our pets. In the next sections of this book, we'll delve even deeper into the benefits of aromatherapy for our beloved pets and explore different recipes and practical tips for incorporating aromatherapy into their daily routine. Stay tuned and get ready to discover more about this exciting topic!

Chapter 3: Importance of Safety in Aromatherapy for Pets

Learn the necessary safety measures and precautions when using essential oils with your pets.

Aromatherapy has gained popularity in recent years as a natural alternative for the well-being of our pets. Essential oils, extracted from plants and herbs, have been shown to have therapeutic properties that can help alleviate different ailments and promote emotional balance in our faithful companions. However, it's essential to consider certain safety measures when using essential oils with our pets.

The first and most important rule of aromatherapy for pets is to understand that dogs and cats are much more sensitive to essential oils than humans. Their sense of smell is extraordinarily acute, which means that the doses and concentration of the oils must be carefully controlled. We should never apply essential oils directly to our pets without diluting them beforehand or without the supervision of an expert in aromatherapy for animals.

Before we start using essential oils, it's critical to research and understand which oils are safe and which ones can be toxic to our furry friends. Some oils, such as tea tree (Tea Tree), eucalyptus and camphor, can be harmful and even cause allergic reactions in animals. Therefore, we must refrain from using oils that have not been specifically recommended for use on pets.

In addition, we must remember that each animal is unique and may react differently to essential oils. For this reason, it is essential to watch our pets carefully when we are applying aromatherapy and to be alert to any signs of discomfort or adverse reactions. If we notice that our pet shows any symptoms of discomfort, such as frequent sneezing, excessive panting, or skin irritation, we should immediately discontinue any application of essential oils and seek the advice of a veterinarian.

Another important precaution is to avoid direct contact of essential oils with the eyes, nose and ears of our pets. These sensitive areas can be irritated or damaged by concentrated oils, causing discomfort and discomfort to our dear furry friends. We must always apply oils safely, diluting the appropriate amounts and avoiding their application near these delicate areas.

It is also necessary to keep in mind that some essential oils can be toxic if ingested by our pets. Therefore, we must ensure that we store the oils in a safe place, out of the reach of our curious pets. If we suspect that our pet has accidentally ingested any essential oil, we should immediately contact our veterinarian for guidance on how to proceed.

These are just some of the basic precautions that we must take into account when using aromatherapy with our pets. The safety and well-being of our faithful companions must always be our priority. In the second half of this chapter, we'll explore in more detail how to select the right oils and how to safely apply them to our pets. Don't miss it! In the second half of this chapter, we'll explore in more detail how to select the right oils and how to safely apply them to our pets. Don't miss it!

When it comes to choosing the right essential oils for our pets, it's important to consider their specific needs and individual sensitivity. Every animal can react differently to different essential oils, so it's critical to conduct thorough research and consult with an expert in animal aromatherapy before starting any treatment.

A safe way to start is to use lavender and chamomile essential oils. These oils are known for their relaxing properties and can be beneficial in relieving stress and anxiety in our pets. In addition, they have also been shown to have anti-inflammatory properties and can help soothe irritated or itchy skin.

When applying essential oils, it is important to dilute them properly to ensure the safety of our pets. Essential oils must be diluted in a carrier oil, such as olive or sweet almond oil, before being applied to the fur or skin of our animals. The recommended dilution for dogs is approximately one drop of essential oil per 20 drops of carrier oil, while for cats, the dilution should be even higher, approximately one drop per 40 drops of carrier oil.

It's important to remember that only small amounts of essential oils should be used on our animals. Less is more when it comes to aromatherapy for pets. An excessive application of essential oils can be harmful and even cause adverse reactions in our furry friends. We should always follow dilution recommendations and apply oils conservatively.

In addition, it is essential to avoid using essential oils near the eyes, nose and ears of our pets, as these sensitive areas can be irritated or damaged. If we want to apply oils to the head area, we must do it very carefully and always properly diluting the oil. For these cases, we can use a cotton ball or our own hands to apply the oil gently and avoid any direct contact with sensitive areas.

When it comes to frequency of use, it's important to remember that less is more. We should not abuse aromatherapy in our pets, as their olfactory system is much more sensitive than ours. The excessive application of essential oils can be overwhelming for our furry friends and cause them discomfort. We recommend starting with brief applications and carefully watching the reaction of our pets. If we notice any signs of discomfort or discomfort, we should stop using the oils immediately.

In short, aromatherapy can be a safe and effective way to promote the well-being of our pets, as long as we take the right precautions. It is essential to carefully research and select the essential oils we will use, dilute them correctly and apply them conservatively. Remember that each animal is unique and can react differently, so we must always be alert to signs of discomfort or adverse reactions. The safety and well-being of our pets must always be our number one priority.

We hope this chapter has given you the tools you need to start using aromatherapy safely and effectively on your pet! In future chapters, we'll further explore how to adapt aromatherapy to different conditions and ailments in our pets. Don't miss it!

Chapter 4: How to Choose the Right Essential Oils for Your Pet

Welcome to chapter 4 of our book, where you will dive into the world of aromatherapy for the well-being of your beloved pet! In this section, you'll learn how to choose the right essential oils to improve the health and well-being of your furry companion. You'll discover what types of oils are safe and beneficial for your pet, providing a natural and harmonious experience.

Before we get into the details, it's essential to understand that not all essential oils are safe for our pets. Like humans, some animals may have special sensitivity or adverse reactions to certain chemical components present in oils. Therefore, we must exercise caution and carefully select the oils that we will use in their care.

The first basic rule is to remember that animals are much more sensitive to essential oils than we are. For this reason, it is always advisable to dilute oils before applying them, and to use moderate amounts. Remember that less is more in the world of aromatherapy for animals. In addition, each animal species can react differently, so it's essential to observe your pet's reactions to a new oil.

Now, what essential oils are safe and beneficial for our adorable pets? Here is a list of some oils that have been shown to have positive properties for your well-being:

1. Lavender: Its relaxing and calming scent can help reduce stress and anxiety in animals. Lavender may also be useful in improving sleep and for relieving insect bites.

2. German Chamomile: Renowned for its anti-inflammatory and soothing properties, German chamomile can be an excellent choice for relieving skin irritation and discomfort caused by allergy.

3. Peppermint: Refreshing mint is ideal for providing instant relief in situations of itchy or upset stomach. However, you must remember that peppermint should be used in very small quantities and use caution if you have a cat, as peppermint essential oils can be irritating to them.

4. Eucalyptus: This oil has antimicrobial properties and can help decongest the respiratory tract. However, you should keep in mind that eucalyptus should not be used on cats, as it can be toxic to them.

5. Tea tree: This oil is known for its antibacterial and antifungal action. It can be useful for treating acne or skin infections. However, remember to dilute it properly and avoid applying it to cats, as their metabolism cannot tolerate it.

In addition to these essential oils, there are many others that can have benefits for our pets. However, it is essential to research and seek professional advice before using new oils. Prevention is always better than cure, so the safety of our furry companions is the most important thing.

Remember, animal lover, that it's crucial to be cautious when starting to use essential oils on your pets. You've made the right choice looking for a natural way to improve their well-being, but remember that every animal is unique and may require different approaches. In the second part of this chapter, we'll explore more options and delve into the practical application of these essential oils. Don't miss the sequel to discover how to get the best results for your pet!

Now that you know some essential oils that are safe and beneficial to your pet, it's important to learn how to apply them correctly. In this second part of the chapter, I'll guide you through the different application methods and give you tips for getting the best results.

1. Massages: Massages are a great way to use essential oils on your pet. Before you begin, be sure to dilute the oil in a safe carrier oil such as coconut oil or sweet almond oil. Then, apply a small amount to your hands and gently massage your pet's body. Pay attention to areas where there may be tension or stiffness, such as the neck or back. Massages not only improve blood circulation, but they also strengthen the bond with your furry friend.

2. Scented baths: Scented baths can be a relaxing and therapeutic experience for your pet. Fill a bathtub or bowl with warm water and add a few drops of diluted essential oil. Make sure the water isn't too hot for your pet. Before you immerse your friend in the water, do a test to make sure the scent isn't too strong or irritating to them. If you notice any discomfort or irritation, rinse it off quickly. Enjoy the bath together and take advantage of this moment to give her a little love and well-being.

3. Scented collars: Scented collars are a great way to provide your pet with the benefits of aromatherapy on an ongoing basis. To create one, buy a fabric or leather necklace and place a few drops of diluted essential oil in it. Make sure the collar is snug but not too tight. This way, your pet can enjoy the positive and relaxing effects of the oil throughout the day.

4. Diffusers: Diffusers are a practical and safe way to scent your home environment and benefit your pet at the same time. Fill the diffuser with water and add a few drops of your chosen essential oil. Turn on the diffuser and allow the scent to disperse throughout the room. Make sure the room is well ventilated so that your pet can enjoy the scent without being exposed to too high a concentration.

5. Pads or washcloths: Pads or washcloths impregnated with diluted essential oils can be used locally to relieve specific discomfort or conditions in your pet. For example, you can apply a warm compress with a few drops of lavender essential oil to painful or inflamed areas to provide relief.

Always remember to observe your pet during and after the application of any essential oil. If you notice any signs of discomfort, irritation, or adverse reaction, discontinue use immediately. Every pet is unique and can react differently to essential oils, so it's essential to be attentive to their needs and respect their limits.

In conclusion, aromatherapy can be a safe and natural way to improve your pet's well-being. With a careful selection of essential oils and proper application, you can provide them with a pleasant and beneficial experience. Don't forget that it's always best to seek professional advice before using new oils and to keep your pet's safety and well-being as a top priority.

Keep exploring the wonderful world of aromatherapy for your pet's well-being and enjoy a more harmonious and healthier relationship with your furry companion!

Chapter 5: Aromatherapy for Pet Stress and Anxiety

Explore how essential oils can help reduce stress and ease anxiety in your pets.

Introduction

Life can be stressful for both humans and animals. In our homes, our pets can also experience stress and anxiety due to various situations. It can be the sound of fireworks during holidays, visits to the vet, the change of environment, the arrival of a new member of the family or even loneliness when we are away.

It's normal to worry about the health and well-being of our beloved pets, and aromatherapy can be a natural and effective tool to help them feel calmer and more balanced. In this chapter, we'll explore how essential oils can help reduce stress and ease anxiety for our beloved pets.

Benefits of aromatherapy for pets

Aromatherapy is an ancient practice that uses the aromas and properties of essential oils to improve health and well-being. These oils, extracted from plants and herbs, contain special components that have positive effects on the body and mind of animals, as well as on human beings.

When used correctly, essential oils can help to calm and relax pets, thereby reducing levels of stress and anxiety. In addition, these oils have properties that can provide emotional support and strengthen the animals' immune system.

Selection of essential oils to reduce stress and relieve anxiety

It's important to remember that every pet is unique and may respond differently to essential oils. Some dogs or cats may enjoy and benefit from certain scents, while others may show a greater preference for different fragrances. Always consider your animal's individual preferences and consult a veterinarian or aromatherapy specialist to make sure you're using the right oils and in the right amount.

There are several essential oils known for their relaxing and calming properties, which can be beneficial for our pets. Next, we will mention some of them:

1. Lavender: This soft, floral fragrance is one of the most popular essential oils used to reduce stress in pets. Its sedative properties can help calm nervous animals and promote a peaceful environment.

2. Chamomile: Known for its calming effect, chamomile is ideal for relieving stress in pets. It can be useful in situations that create anxiety or when there is a change in your environment.

3. Bergamot: With its refreshing citrus scent, bergamot can help relieve tension and anxiety in pets. It is a great emotional support for those animals that feel insecure or fearful.

4. Vetiver: This essential oil has relaxing properties and can be beneficial in helping pets overcome stressful situations. It helps to create a calm and peaceful environment.

Keep in mind that these are just a few examples of essential oils that can help reduce stress and ease your pets' anxiety. It's essential to do more research on each oil and understand the possible side effects before using them on your animals.

So far, we've explored how essential oils can be a natural and effective tool for reducing stress and alleviating anxiety in our pets. In the second half of this chapter, we'll discover how to properly use essential oils and how to safely apply them to our beloved furry companions. Don't miss it! Selecting Essential Oils to Reduce Stress and Relieve Anxiety (Continued)

5. Ylang-ylang: This essential oil has a sweet, floral scent that can help calm stressed or anxious pets. Its relaxing effect can be beneficial during times of intense stress or changes in the environment.

6. Peppermint: Although peppermint is known for its stimulating effect on humans, in small doses it can have a calming effect on pets. It helps to refresh the mind and relax the muscles, especially in stressful situations.

7. Rose: The sweet scent of rose can help create a calm and relaxing environment for pets. This essential oil is especially useful in situations of anxiety or fear, allowing animals to feel more secure and calm.

Remember that the appropriate amount and the form of application may vary depending on the pet and the situation in which it is located. It is essential to dilute essential oils in a carrier oil, such as almond or jojoba oil, before using them on your animals. Also, avoid applying essential oils directly to your pet's skin and make sure they don't ingest the mixtures.

Additional Tips for Using Aromatherapy on Your Pets

Here are some additional tips for using aromatherapy safely and effectively on your pets:

1. Consult a veterinarian or aromatherapy specialist: Before starting any treatment, it's important to get expert advice. They can recommend the right essential oils for your pet and provide you with specific dosage and application guidelines.

2. Watch your pet's reaction: each animal is unique and may have different reactions to essential oils. Watch how your pet responds to scents and adjust the amount accordingly. If you notice any signs of discomfort or allergic reaction, discontinue use and consult a veterinarian.

3. Use aromatic diffusers or collars: these dispersion methods allow scents to be distributed smoothly and consistently in your pet's environment. They can help create a relaxing environment and promote calm.

4. Avoid overuse: Remember that balance is the key to aromatherapy. There is no need to saturate the environment with essential oils. Use them moderately and at specific times of stress or anxiety.

5. Keep essential oils out of reach of your pets: Make sure to store essential oils in a safe place, away from your pet's reach. Some oils can be toxic if ingested in large quantities.

Congratulations! Now you have a list of essential oils that can help reduce stress and ease anxiety in your pets, as well as some tips for using them safely. Remember that aromatherapy is a complementary tool, and it's always important to consult an animal health professional before implementing any treatment.

Chapter 6: Benefits of Aromatherapy in Caring for Your Pet's Skin

Learn how to use essential oils to naturally improve and maintain the health of your pet's skin.

The skin is one of the most important organs in the body of our dear furry friends. In addition to being the first protective barrier against external agents, it also reflects the general health of our pet. That's why it's vital to pay attention to and properly care for the skin of our animal companions.

In this chapter, we're going to explore the benefits of aromatherapy in caring for your pet's skin. Aromatherapy is an ancient practice that uses essential oils extracted from plants to improve physical and emotional well-being. These essential oils have therapeutic properties that can help treat different skin conditions of your pet naturally and safely.

One of the greatest benefits of aromatherapy is its ability to soothe and relieve skin irritations. Some essential oils, such as lavender and chamomile, are known for their anti-inflammatory and relaxing properties. These oils can help reduce irritation, redness, and itching on your pet's skin. In addition, its calming effect can also be beneficial for those animals that suffer from stress or anxiety, since skin and emotional state are closely related.

Another important point to highlight is the antimicrobial power of certain essential oils. Some, such as tea tree and lemongrass, have antibacterial and antifungal properties, making them natural allies to combat skin infections. These oils can help keep your pet's skin free of harmful bacteria and fungi, promoting healthy, problem-free skin.

In addition to soothing irritations and fighting infections, aromatherapy can help moisturize and nourish your pet's skin. Some essential oils contain compounds that help retain moisture and improve skin elasticity. For example, rosehip oil and jojoba oil are known for their moisturizing and rejuvenating properties. These oils can be especially beneficial for animals whose skin is dry and dehydrated, providing them with the necessary hydration for healthy, glowing skin.

It's important to note that when using aromatherapy to care for your pet's skin, you must do so safely and with caution. Not all essential oils are safe for animals, and some can be toxic if improperly applied. It is always recommended to consult a veterinarian specializing in aromatherapy before starting to use essential oils on your pet. They can guide you in the right choice of oils according to the needs of your animal companion and offer you the right doses to avoid any possible adverse effects.

In short, aromatherapy can be a natural and effective option to improve and maintain the health of your pet's skin. Its anti-inflammatory, antimicrobial and moisturizing properties can help relieve irritation, fight infections and provide healthy, radiant skin. Always remember to have the guidance of a veterinarian specializing in aromatherapy to ensure the proper and safe use of essential oils in your pet.

Don't miss the chance to discover more tips and benefits of aromatherapy in the next chapter, where we'll explore how to select and apply essential oils properly. Get ready to unravel the secrets behind healthy, happy skin for your faithful four-legged companion. Taking care of your pet's skin is crucial to their overall health and well-being. In the first half of this chapter, we explored some benefits of aromatherapy in caring for your furry companion's skin. Now, we'll continue to discover more tips and benefits so you can get the most out of this natural practice.

A fundamental aspect of caring for your pet's skin is to keep it clean and free of dirt. Aromatherapy can be of great help in this regard, as some essential oils have disinfectant and cleansing properties. Essential oils such as eucalyptus and tea tree are known for their purifying effects, which can help remove bacteria and dirt from your pet's skin. You can dilute a few drops of these oils in water and use it as a cleansing spray for your coat and skin. Always remember to consult a specialized veterinarian for the appropriate recommendations and the correct dilution measurements.

In addition to keeping your skin clean, it's important to provide it with the nutrients it needs for healthy skin. Some essential oils contain vitamins and antioxidants that can help nourish your pet's skin. For example, carrot essential oil is rich in vitamin A, which is essential for skin regeneration. Geranium essential oil, on the other hand, contains antioxidant properties that can help protect the skin from damage caused by free radicals. You can add a few drops of these essential oils to a carrier oil, such as coconut oil, and gently massage your pet's coat and skin. This massage will not only promote the absorption of nutrients, but it will also strengthen the bond between you and your pet.

Another aspect to consider when caring for your pet's skin is the control of fleas and ticks. These parasites can cause irritation, itching, and even transmit diseases to your pet. Aromatherapy can be a natural and effective alternative to repel and control these pests. Some essential oils, such as citronella and catnip, are known for their ability to repel these insects. You can dilute a few drops of these essential oils in water and use it as a repellent spray. Make sure to avoid contact with your pet's eyes and mucous membranes, as some essential oils can irritate these sensitive areas. As always, consult a specialized veterinarian for appropriate application recommendations and necessary precautions.

Last but not least, aromatherapy can be a useful tool for keeping your pet calm and emotionally balanced. Stress and anxiety can affect your skin's health, causing irritation and dermatological problems. Some essential oils, such as sandalwood and Roman chamomile, are known for their relaxing and calming effects. You can add a few drops of these oils to an aroma diffuser specially designed for pets or use scented collars or pillows. Remember that pets are sensitive to odors, so you should always make sure that the essential oils you use are safe and suitable for them. Once again, the guidance of a veterinarian specializing in aromatherapy is essential to ensure the safety of your pet.

In conclusion, aromatherapy can be a valuable tool for improving and maintaining the health of your pet's skin. From cleansing and disinfecting the skin to providing nutrients and controlling pests, essential oils can offer a natural and effective solution. Always remember to consult a specialized veterinarian before using essential oils on your pet, to ensure that they are safe and appropriate for the individual needs of your animal companion.

I hope you enjoyed this chapter on the benefits of aromatherapy in caring for your pet's skin. In the next chapter, we'll explore how to select and apply essential oils appropriately. Continue to discover the secrets behind healthy, glowing skin for your faithful furry friend. Don't miss it.

Chapter 7: Aromatherapy to ease digestive distress in pets

Learn how essential oils can alleviate common digestive problems in pets.

Digestive health is essential to ensure the well-being of our beloved pets. Just as we humans sometimes experience stomach discomfort, our pets can also be affected by digestive problems. However, did you know that aromatherapy can be a natural and effective option to relieve these discomforts?

Aromatherapy uses essential oils, highly concentrated plant substances that have been used for centuries for their therapeutic benefits. These powerful oils have healing properties and can be a valuable tool to take care of the health of our pets naturally.

One of the most common digestive problems in pets is indigestion. Many times, our furry friends can suffer from stomach upset due to inadequate nutrition, changes in diet, or even because they eat something they shouldn't. In these cases, essential oils can provide relief.

Peppermint essential oil, for example, is known for its ability to calm the stomach and relieve symptoms of indigestion in pets. It's refreshing scent and antispasmodic properties can help relax stomach muscles and promote better digestion. If you notice that your pet is showing signs of an upset stomach, dilute a drop of peppermint essential oil in water and apply it gently to their fur or abdominal area.

Another common digestive problem is flatulence, a topic that can be uncomfortable for both our pets and us. However, essential oils can offer effective relief for this gastrointestinal problem.

Ginger essential oil, renowned for its carminative properties, can help reduce gas production and relieve abdominal distention in our pets. It's warm, spicy scent is not only pleasant, but it also stimulates blood circulation and the digestive system. To use it, dilute a drop of ginger essential oil in a vegetable carrier oil and gently massage your pet's abdomen.

In addition to indigestion and flatulence, there are other common digestive problems affecting our pets, such as constipation and diarrhea. These disorders can be uncomfortable and painful for our furry friends, but aromatherapy offers natural solutions to alleviate them.

Chamomile essential oil, known for its anti-inflammatory and soothing properties, can help soften stools and promote bowel regularity. Its sweet, relaxing scent can also reduce the anxiety associated with these problems. To use it, dilute a drop of chamomile essential oil in a vegetable carrier oil and gently massage your pet's abdominal area in circular motions.

In conclusion, aromatherapy can be a natural alternative to relieve digestive distress in our pets. Essential oils, such as peppermint, ginger and chamomile, offer therapeutic benefits that can promote better digestive health. However, it's important to remember that every pet is unique, so it's essential to consult a veterinarian before using essential oils, especially if your pet has a pre-existing health condition.

Now, I invite you to discover in the second part of this chapter how to use essential oils safely and effectively to relieve digestive distress in your beloved pets. A natural solution that will surprise you! When using aromatherapy to relieve digestive distress in our pets, it's important to consider some considerations to ensure their safety and effectiveness. In this second part of the chapter, I'll show you how to use essential oils safely and effectively, as well as some additional precautions.

Before starting aromatherapy, it's critical to remember that every pet is unique and may react differently to essential oils. For this reason, a sensitivity test is necessary before applying any oil to your pet.

To perform this test, dilute a small amount of essential oil in a vegetable carrier oil, such as coconut or jojoba oil. Apply a small amount of this diluted mixture to an area of your pet's skin and watch their reaction for the next 24 hours. If there are no signs of irritation or discomfort, it's safe to proceed with using that oil.

Once you've determined which essential oil is safe for your pet, you can start using it to ease their digestive distress.

To deal with indigestion, for example, you can create a diluted blend of peppermint essential oil with a vegetable carrier oil. Gently apply this mixture to your pet's coat, especially in their abdominal area. Massage this area in circular motions and let the refreshing scent of peppermint oil soothe your stomach.

If your pet is suffering from flatulence, ginger essential oil can be of great help. Dilute a drop of this oil in a vegetable carrier oil and gently massage your pet's abdomen. The warm, spicy scent of ginger will stimulate blood circulation and help relieve abdominal distention.

In case of constipation or diarrhea, chamomile essential oil can be an effective option. Dilute a drop of this oil in a vegetable carrier oil and gently massage your pet's abdominal area in circular motions. Chamomile has anti-inflammatory and soothing properties that can soften stools and promote bowel regularity.

Remember that aromatherapy should be used as a complement to appropriate veterinary treatment. If your pet's digestive distress persists or worsens, it's important to seek the care of a veterinary professional.

In addition, it's crucial to note that not all essential oils are safe for pets. Some oils, such as citrus or tea tree, can be toxic to animals. For this reason, you should always consult a veterinarian before using any essential oil on your pet, especially if it has a pre-existing health condition.

In conclusion, aromatherapy can be a natural and effective option to relieve digestive distress in our pets. Peppermint, ginger and chamomile essential oils offer therapeutic benefits that can promote better digestive health. Remember to perform a sensitivity test before using any oil and consult a veterinarian to ensure the safety and effectiveness of aromatherapy for your pet.

Chapter 8: Aromatherapy for your pet's respiratory well-being

The respiratory health of our beloved pets is essential to their overall well-being. Just like us, animals can experience respiratory problems that affect their quality of life. Fortunately, aromatherapy can be a powerful ally in caring for your pet's respiratory health, helping them breathe better and alleviating problems such as nasal congestion.

The use of essential oils in aromatherapy has been recognized for their therapeutic benefits in both humans and animals. Essential oils are natural plant extracts that contain volatile chemical compounds with medicinal properties. These compounds can be used to safely and effectively improve your pet's respiratory health.

It's important to note that while some essential oils may be beneficial to humans, not all of them are safe for application to animals. Before you start using aromatherapy on your pet, it's essential to carefully research and select the right essential oils for your pet. In addition, you must consider their species, size, and possible pre-existing health conditions.

To improve your pet's respiratory health and alleviate problems such as nasal congestion, it is recommended to use certain essential oils known for their decongestant and anti-inflammatory properties. Some safe and effective options include eucalyptus, lavender, and peppermint essential oil.

Eucalyptus essential oil is especially useful for relieving nasal congestion in pets. Its expectorant and decongestant properties help to clean the respiratory tract, making breathing easier. You can use it in diffusers or add a few drops diluted in warm water to create a solution that your pet can inhale.

Lavender, on the other hand, has anti-inflammatory and relaxing properties. If your pet is suffering from respiratory problems caused by inflammation of the respiratory tract, lavender can go a long way in alleviating that discomfort. You can dilute a few drops of lavender essential oil in a carrier oil and gently massage your pet's chest.

Finally, peppermint is a refreshing and decongestant essential oil that can help relieve nasal congestion in your pet. Its stimulating scent and decongestant properties can make breathing easier and provide relief. As with other essential oils, it's important to pre-dilute it and use it properly and safely.

Remember that before using any essential oil on your pet, it is essential to research and consult a holistic veterinarian or aromatherapy expert to obtain the appropriate recommendations for their species and specific condition. Every pet is unique and may react differently to essential oils, so it's important to take precautions and use them safely.

In the second part of this chapter, we'll further explore how to use these essential oils to improve your pet's respiratory health and provide detailed guidance on proper application and dosage. Get ready to discover how aromatherapy can be the natural path to your pet's respiratory well-being. You can't miss it!

In the second part of this chapter, we will delve into the specific use of the essential oils mentioned above for your pet's respiratory well-being. We'll learn more about how to apply them safely and effectively to relieve respiratory problems and promote the overall health of your faithful companion.

Let's start with eucalyptus essential oil. A popular choice for relieving nasal congestion in pets, this oil is known for its expectorant and decongestant properties. To use it, dilute a few drops of eucalyptus essential oil in a carrier oil, such as coconut or almond oil. Then, gently massage your pet's chest with this mixture, paying special attention to the area where the trachea and lungs are located. The massage will help the active compounds in the oil penetrate your pet's respiratory system, providing relief and making it easier for them to breathe.

Let's now move on to lavender, an essential oil that not only has anti-inflammatory properties, but also relaxing effects. If your pet suffers from respiratory problems caused by inflammation of the respiratory tract, lavender can be a natural ally. To apply it, dilute a few drops of lavender essential oil in a carrier oil and gently massage your pet's chest. This massage will help reduce inflammation and calm any discomfort you may be experiencing. In addition, the relaxing scent of lavender can help your pet feel calm and, in an environment, conducive to healing.

Finally, let's talk about peppermint essential oil. With its refreshing scent and decongestant properties, peppermint can be a great help in relieving nasal congestion in your pet. To use it, dilute a few drops of peppermint essential oil in a carrier oil and gently massage your pet's chest. You can also add a few drops of peppermint essential oil to a diffuser or vaporizer in the area where your pet spends most of its time. The stimulating scent of peppermint will help to decongest your respiratory tract and provide immediate relief.

Remember that every pet is unique and may react differently to essential oils. It is essential to observe your pet during and after the application of essential oils to ensure that there are no negative reactions. If you notice any signs of discomfort or irritation, discontinue use and consult a holistic veterinarian or aromatherapy expert.

To conclude, aromatherapy can be a natural and effective way to improve your pet's respiratory health. Eucalyptus, lavender and peppermint essential oils can be valuable tools for relieving nasal congestion and other respiratory problems. Always remember to carefully research and select the right essential oils for your pet, taking into account their species, size and pre-existing health conditions.

Your pet's respiratory well-being is essential to their quality of life, and with the help of aromatherapy, you can provide them with the relief and care they deserve. Explore beyond the conventional and discover how essential oils can make a difference in the health of your faithful companion!

Chapter 9: Aromatherapy for Pain and Inflammation Relief in Pets

Explore how essential oils can naturally help reduce pain and inflammation in your pet.

When our beloved furry companions suffer from physical ailments, it's natural to want to find ways to ease their pain and discomfort. Fortunately, aromatherapy can offer a natural and effective solution to help relieve pain and inflammation in our pets.

Aromatherapy is an ancient practice that uses the aromas of essential oils extracted from plants, flowers and herbs to improve physical and emotional well-being. These oils contain biochemical compounds that have therapeutic properties, and when inhaled or applied topically, they can provide relief to a variety of health problems.

When treating pain and inflammation in pets, it's important to remember that not all essential oils are safe to use. Some plants and oils can be toxic to our furry friends, so it's essential to consult a veterinarian or aromatherapist specializing in pet care before starting any treatment.

Fortunately, there are several safe and highly effective essential oils that can be used to relieve pain and inflammation in pets. One of the most popular oils for this purpose is lavender essential oil. This oil has been used for centuries for its analgesic and anti-inflammatory qualities. Applying it properly, it can help relieve muscle and joint pain in our pets, promoting their overall well-being.

Another essential oil beneficial for pain relief is chamomile essential oil. This oil is known for its anti-inflammatory and soothing properties, especially when it comes to skin conditions such as dermatitis or insect bites. In addition to reducing inflammation, it can help ease discomfort and accelerate the healing process.

Peppermint essential oil may also be helpful in relieving pain and inflammation in pets. Peppermint is known for its analgesic and refreshing properties, making it an ideal option for treating muscle and joint pain. However, it is important to properly dilute the oil before use, as it can be irritating to the skin of our pets if used in high concentrations.

The way these essential oils are used can vary depending on the type of pet and the ailment you want to treat. In some cases, it may be more effective to use them in the form of massages, diluted in a base oil such as coconut oil or jojoba oil. In other cases, inhalation through a diffuser or application to collars or bandages may be more appropriate.

Before starting any treatment, it's important to research and educate yourself about essential oils, their properties, and their potential side effects on pets. In addition, it is crucial to respect the recommended doses and to be attentive to any signs of discomfort or allergic reaction in our pet.

In short, aromatherapy can be an effective and natural tool for relieving pain and inflammation in our beloved pets. Essential oils such as lavender, chamomile and peppermint can provide remarkable relief, but we must always make sure that we use them properly and in the right doses. In the second part of this chapter, we'll explore more beneficial essential oils and how to use them to provide well-being for our pets. Keep reading to discover more aromatic surprises! The second half of this chapter focuses on other beneficial essential oils and how to use them to provide well-being for our pets. In addition to lavender, chamomile and peppermint, there are other natural options that can help relieve pain and inflammation in our furry companions.

A very popular and safe essential oil is ginger oil. This oil has powerful anti-inflammatory and analgesic properties, making it an excellent choice for treating muscle and joint pain in pets. By gently applying oil diluted in a base oil, such as sweet almond, we can stimulate blood circulation and reduce inflammation in affected areas.

Another beneficial essential oil is tea tree essential oil. Known for its antibacterial and anti-inflammatory properties, this oil can be especially useful in treating skin infections, insect bites and minor injuries in our pets. By diluting a few drops in warm water and applying it as a compress or vaporizer, we can help ease the pain and accelerate the healing process.

In addition to these essential oils, others such as rosemary, eucalyptus and frankincense essential oils can also be beneficial in relieving pain and inflammation in pets. Rosemary essential oil has analgesic and stimulating properties, and may be useful for improving blood circulation and relieving muscle pain. Eucalyptus essential oil, on the other hand, has expectorant and anti-inflammatory qualities, which can be beneficial in cases of respiratory congestion and respiratory problems. Finally, frankincense essential oil has been used for centuries for its anti-inflammatory and immune-supporting properties. By mixing these essential oils with a suitable base oil, such as olive or sunflower oil, we can create a gentle mixture and use it to massage our pets.

When using these essential oils, it is important to always remember to dilute them properly and to respect the recommended doses. Every pet is unique and may respond differently to essential oils, so it's critical to be on the lookout for any signs of discomfort or allergic reaction. It is always advisable to perform a sensitivity test before using any essential oil on our pets, applying a small amount diluted to a small area of the skin and observing any reaction for at least 24 hours.

In addition to topical application, inhaling essential oils can be beneficial for relieving pain and inflammation in pets. Using an appropriate aromatherapy diffuser and following the instructions for use can help our furry companions breathe the therapeutic benefits of essential oils. However, it's important to remember that some essential oils can be toxic to pets if inhaled at high concentrations, so we must always ensure that we use safe essential oils and dilute them properly.

In conclusion, aromatherapy can be a natural and effective way to relieve pain and inflammation in our pets. Essential oils such as lavender, chamomile, peppermint, ginger, tea tree, rosemary, eucalyptus and frankincense can offer remarkable benefits to the well-being of our furry companions. However, it is essential to always consult a veterinarian or aromatherapist specializing in pet care before starting any treatment, to ensure the safety and well-being of our beloved animals.

I hope you enjoyed this exploration of aromatherapy for the relief of pain and inflammation in pets. Keep discovering the wonderful world of essential oils and how they can improve the quality of life of your beloved furry companions. Never stop learning and experimenting with the wonders of nature for the well-being of your pets!

Chapter 10:
Aromatherapy for
Emotional Support for
Pets

L earn how essential oils can help balance your pets' emotions, promoting their emotional well-being.

In the exciting world of aromatherapy, essential oils have been shown to not only benefit human beings, but can also have a positive impact on the emotional well-being of our beloved pets. If you've ever wondered how, you can help your four-legged companion find emotional balance, you've come to the right chapter!

Emotions play a crucial role in the lives of our pets. Just like us, they experience joy, fear, sadness, and stress. It's our responsibility as owners to understand and address the emotional needs of our furry friends. This is where aromatherapy comes into play.

Aromatherapy is a therapeutic practice that uses the powers of essential oils to promote health and well-being. These oils are natural volatile compounds extracted from plants and have been used for centuries because of their healing properties. Thanks to their aromatic nature and therapeutic benefits, essential oils can help our pets find a state of calm and balance.

There are different ways to use aromatherapy with your pets. One of them is through the diffusion of essential oils into the environment. Oils, such as lavender or geranium, can be dispersed in the air to create a soft and relaxing fragrance. This technique is ideal for times of stress, such as thunderstorms or visits to the vet.

Another way to use aromatherapy is through massages with diluted essential oils. Before applying any oil to your pet's skin, make sure it's safe and species-appropriate. Some oils, such as tea tree or lemon, can be toxic to certain animals. Always follow the recommendations of an aromatherapy expert to ensure your pet's safety.

Essential oil massages can help calm anxiety and improve your pet's mood. In addition to providing a deep sense of relaxation, essential oils can stimulate your furry companion's senses, creating a unique sensory experience.

Always remember to watch your pet's reaction to essential oils. Every animal is unique and may respond differently to fragrances. If you notice any signs of discomfort or allergic reaction, discontinue use immediately.

Aromatherapy for emotional support for pets is a wonderful tool that can help improve the quality of life of our beloved four-legged friends. By providing a relaxing and restorative environment, we can help our pets find an emotional balance that allows them to live full and happy lives.

In the second half of this chapter, we'll further explore the benefits of aromatherapy in emotional support for pets, discovering which essential oils are safe and effective for different emotional situations. Get ready to dive into the fascinating world of aromatherapy and delve deeper into how you can help your pet find the calm and serenity they so deserve.

Remember, keep reading carefully and you'll discover how scents can transform the emotional life of your faithful companion. Don't miss it! In the second half of this chapter, we'll delve into the specific benefits of aromatherapy for emotional support for pets, focusing on different situations and moods that can affect our furry friends.

When it comes to separation anxiety, many pet owners face the challenge of leaving their beloved companions when they leave home. Aromatherapy can be an effective solution to help calm animals that experience this type of anxiety. Some essential oils recommended for this purpose are lavender, chamomile and vetiver. These oils can help relax your pet and create a peaceful environment before going out.

If your pet suffers from fear or stress during thunderstorms or other stressful situations, aromatherapy can also help. Cedarwood, lavender and sweet orange essential oils can be especially beneficial for calming pets in times of tension. You can dilute these oils in water and use them in a diffuser to create a relaxing atmosphere at home.

For those animals that may have difficulty relaxing or sleeping, essential oils such as Roman chamomile, lavender and ylang ylang may be helpful. You can use these oils in a diffuser or apply a small amount diluted with water to your bed to help promote peaceful sleep.

It's important to remember that aromatherapy isn't a one-size-fits-all solution to the emotional needs of pets and that every animal is unique. Some essential oils may not be safe for certain species, or they may affect some pets differently. It's always a good idea to consult an aromatherapy expert before using essential oils on your pets.

In addition to using the essential oils mentioned above, there are other ways to incorporate aromatherapy into your pet's daily life. You can use them during relaxing massage sessions or add a few drops to a water solution to spray your rest area and create a relaxing environment.

Always remember to watch your pet's reaction to essential oils and watch for any signs of discomfort or allergic reaction. If at any time you notice any problems, stop using the oils immediately and seek veterinary attention if necessary.

Aromatherapy can be a valuable tool for emotional support for your pets, helping them find a state of calm and balance in stressful situations. By dedicating time and attention to your furry companion's emotional needs, you can improve their quality of life and promote their overall well-being.

In conclusion, aromatherapy offers pet owners a natural and effective way to help their furry friends find calm and emotional balance. Through the proper use of safe and effective essential oils, you can provide your pet with a supportive environment that promotes their emotional well-being.

Don't miss the chance to discover how essential oils can transform your pet's life and improve their quality of life! Stay committed to caring for and loving your beloved four-legged companion, and together you'll enjoy a stronger, more balanced relationship.

Keep exploring the wonderful world of aromatherapy and see how this practice can improve your pet's emotional well-being!

Chapter 11:
Aromatherapy for flea and
tick management in pets

Learn how to use essential oils as natural flea and tick repellents on your pets.

Fleas and ticks are common problems affecting our beloved pets. These parasites can cause discomfort, itching, infections, and serious illnesses if not treated properly. Fortunately, there is a natural alternative to help repel them: aromatherapy.

Aromatherapy uses the therapeutic benefits of essential oils extracted from plants to promote physical and emotional well-being. These concentrated vegetable oils contain natural chemical compounds that can effectively ward off fleas and ticks from your pets.

By using the right essential oils and applying them correctly, you can protect your pet from these parasites without resorting to harsh chemicals. Here's a guide to using aromatherapy as a natural solution for flea and tick management.

1. Choose the right essential oils

There are several essential oils that are known for their insect-repellent properties. Some of the most effective at repelling fleas and ticks include citronella oil, tea tree oil, and lavender oil. These oils have a pleasant scent for humans but unpleasant for parasites, keeping them away from pets.

It's important to note that not all essential oils are safe for pets. Some can be toxic if ingested or applied directly to the skin without dilution.

Always make sure you get high-quality essential oils and dilute them properly before use on your pets.

2. Prepare a diluted solution

Once you've selected safe and effective essential oils, you'll need to dilute them in a base oil or water before applying them to your pet. This is especially important to avoid skin irritation and to ensure that the oils are safe to use.

A common dilution is to mix 5 to 10 drops of essential oil into an ounce of base oil, such as fractionated coconut oil or sweet almond oil. You can also mix diluted essential oils with distilled water, using a base of one part diluted essential oil and three parts waters.

3. Apply the solution at strategic points

Once you've prepared the diluted solution, it's time to apply it to your pet. Remember to do it gently and never in sensitive areas, such as the eyes, ears or nose.

Apply the solution to strategic points on your pet's body, such as the neck, behind the ears, at the base of the tail and on the legs. These areas are the places where fleas and ticks usually begin to infest.

In addition, you can add a few drops of the diluted solution to a collar for your pet to wear. This will help maintain constant and long-term protection against fleas and ticks.

Remember that aromatherapy is not a substitute for regular flea and tick treatments, especially if your pet is already infested. Always consult your veterinarian to get the best parasite control plan for your pet.

With aromatherapy, you now have a natural and safe option to protect your pet from the discomfort caused by fleas and ticks. Get ready to discover in the next installment how to make the most of this wonderful tool and more tips to keep your pet free of these annoying parasites.

It will continue... 4. Use the diluted solution with caution

Now that you've prepared the diluted essential oil solution, it's important to use it with caution. Remember that animals have a much more developed sense of smell than ours, so you should make sure you don't use an excessive amount of the solution, as it could be overwhelming for your pet.

Apply the diluted solution gently to your pet's coat, avoiding direct contact with the skin. Do gentle massages to ensure that the solution is distributed evenly. If your pet is uncomfortable or has an adverse reaction, discontinue use immediately and consult your veterinarian.

It's important to note that aromatherapy shouldn't be the only measure you take to protect your pet against fleas and ticks. You should continue with the regular treatments recommended by your veterinarian and maintain a clean, parasite-free environment.

5. Other tips for managing fleas and ticks

In addition to using aromatherapy, there are other steps you can take to minimize the presence of fleas and ticks on your pet and in your home.

Keep your pet away from infested areas, such as tall lawns, fields, or woods. These are places where parasites are usually present to a greater extent. If you're returning from a walk or walk, thoroughly check your pet for fleas and ticks, and carefully remove them using special tweezers.

Wash your pet's bedding regularly and vacuum and clean your home regularly. These actions will help eliminate flea and tick eggs and larvae that may have settled in the environment.

6. Consult your vet.

Remember that every pet is unique and what works for one may not work for another. It is always advisable to consult your veterinarian before implementing any type of natural treatment, including aromatherapy, especially if your pet has a pre-existing health condition.

Your veterinarian will be able to provide specific guidance on the right essential oils for your pet, safe doses, and any additional precautions you should consider.

In conclusion, aromatherapy can be a natural and safe alternative to help repel fleas and ticks from your pets. However, it's important to use it with caution and in conjunction with other parasite control methods recommended by your veterinarian.

Remember that your pet's well-being is a responsibility that you must take seriously. With aromatherapy, you now have an additional tool to keep your beloved four-legged companions free of fleas and ticks.

We hope this guide has been useful to you and that you find aromatherapy a natural and effective way to care for your pet. Continue to explore and learn about other benefits of aromatherapy in the next chapter!

Remember, your pet's well-being is in your hands. Until the next installment!

It will continue...

Chapter 12:
Aromatherapy for the care of your pet's coat

Our pets' fur is an important part of their appearance and overall health. A shiny, soft coat is not only pleasing to the eye, but also indicates overall well-being in our beloved pets. That's why in this chapter, we'll explore the benefits of aromatherapy for caring for your pet's coat.

Aromatherapy has been used for centuries to promote human health and well-being, but did you know that it can also be beneficial for our furry friends? Essential oils extracted from plants and herbs have healing and soothing properties that can help improve the condition of your pet's coat and contribute to their overall well-being.

One of the main benefits of aromatherapy for coat care is its ability to strengthen and nourish your pet's hair. Some essential oils, such as lavender and rosemary, stimulate hair growth and help prevent excessive hair loss. These essential oils can also relieve itchiness and skin irritation, which is especially beneficial for pets with dermatological problems.

In addition to strengthening the coat, aromatherapy can help keep it clean and free of bad odors. Most essential oils have antifungal and antibacterial properties, meaning they can prevent the proliferation of microorganisms that cause bad odors and skin diseases. For example, tea tree essential oil is known for its antifungal and antibacterial effects, and is widely used to prevent infections in pet fur.

However, before you start using essential oils to care for your pet's coat, it's important to consider some precautions. Not all essential oils are safe for topical use in pets, and some can be toxic if ingested. It's crucial to research and consult a veterinarian before using any essential oil on your pet.

When using aromatherapy to care for your pet's coat, always remember to dilute the essential oil in a base oil such as jojoba or sweet almond. Also, consider your pet's individual sensitivity and start with small amounts to observe any adverse reactions. If you notice any signs of irritation or discomfort, stop using the essential oil immediately and seek professional guidance.

In short, aromatherapy can be a natural and effective option to improve the health and appearance of your pet's coat. Essential oils have strengthening, nourishing and cleansing properties that can promote a shiny, healthy coat.

Continue exploring the different ways to use aromatherapy to care for your pet's coat in the second half of this chapter, where we'll present you with some recipes and practical tips to get the most out of the benefits of essential oils. Get ready to discover how you can naturally further improve your pet's beauty and well-being. Let's continue our journey together!

Once you've taken the necessary precautions and consulted with your veterinarian, it's time to continue exploring how you can use aromatherapy to care for your pet's coat.

Another benefit of aromatherapy is its ability to calm and relax your pet while bathing or brushing. With reduced stress and anxiety, your pet will be more willing to enjoy these moments and experience less discomfort. Some essential oils that can help soothe your pet during coat care are chamomile and mandarin oil. Simply add a few drops to a damp cloth or brush and gently caress your pet's coat to release the relaxing benefits of these oils.

In addition to adding essential oils during bathing, you can also create your own aromatic spray to refresh your pet's coat between baths. The most common blend includes distilled water, witch hazel, and essential oils of your choice. Prepare a spray bottle and spray gently on your pet's coat, avoiding the eye and mouth area. This will help keep your pet's coat fresh and smelling nice.

Some additional recipes you can try to care for your pet's coat are:

1. Lavender essential oil and coconut oil: Mix a few drops of lavender essential oil with a spoonful of coconut oil to create a nourishing lotion for your pet's coat. This mixture will help moisturize and soften the coat, leaving it shiny and healthy.

2. Lemon essential oil and distilled water: Mix a few drops of lemon essential oil in distilled water and use this solution as a final rinse after bathing. The lemon will help to eliminate the smell and keep the coat fresh longer.

3. Tea Tree Essential Oil and Jojoba Oil: Mix a few drops of tea tree essential oil into jojoba oil and use this to massage your pet's scalp. This blend will help relieve itching and irritation, promoting a healthy, problem-free coat.

Always remember to observe your pet during and after the application of essential oils to ensure that there are no adverse reactions. It's always best to start with small amounts and gradually increase if necessary.

In conclusion, aromatherapy can be a powerful tool for improving the health and appearance of your pet's coat. Essential oils are a natural and effective way to strengthen, nourish and cleanse the coat, while providing relaxing and soothing benefits. Don't hesitate to experiment with different mixes and find the ones that work best for your pet.

Enjoy this wellness journey with your beloved pet and make the most of the benefits of aromatherapy in caring for their fur!

Chapter 13:
Aromatherapy for the Relief of Separation Anxiety in Pets

Learn to use essential oils to calm the anxiety your pet feels when you are separated from them.

In the wonderful world of pets, our dear companions, we sometimes find ourselves faced with situations where we must separate ourselves from them. Whether for work, social or personal reasons, it is inevitable that at some point we will have to leave them alone at home. However, when our animals experience separation anxiety, that time can become stressful for both them and us.

Separation anxiety is a common disorder in pets and is manifested through unwanted behaviors such as excessive barking, relieving themselves in inappropriate places, destroying objects or being restless. These behaviors are a natural response to the fear and distress they feel when separated from their owners. Fortunately, there is a natural and effective solution to help ease this anxiety: aromatherapy.

Aromatherapy is an ancient practice that uses the aromas and therapeutic properties of essential oils extracted from aromatic plants to promote physical and emotional well-being. These essential oils can be used safely on our pets, as long as the proper instructions are followed.

When it comes to calming separation anxiety in pets, there are a number of essential oils that are especially beneficial. One of them is lavender essential oil. This oil is known for its relaxing and sedative properties. When used in a diffuser or an aromatic collar suitable for pets, the soft scent of lavender can have a calming effect on your furry companion, helping them to relax and feel calmer during your absence.

Another essential oil effective for relieving separation anxiety in pets is chamomile essential oil. Chamomile is known for its anti-stress and calming properties, making it an excellent choice to help your pet stay calm when you're not around. You can dilute a few drops of chamomile essential oil in water and use it to spray the environment where your animal spends most of its time. You can also apply a small amount of oil directly to their fur (making sure they don't lick it) to enjoy the soothing benefits of this wonderful essential oil.

In addition to lavender and chamomile, there are other essential oils that can help calm separation anxiety in pets, such as vetiver, bergamot or ylang-ylang. However, it's important to remember that aromatherapy isn't a magic solution and every animal is unique. Some pets may respond differently to certain essential oils, so it's essential to see how your four-legged companion reacts to their use and adjust the dose or try other oils if necessary.

In this chapter, we've explored how aromatherapy can be an effective tool for alleviating separation anxiety in pets. Essential oils, such as lavender and chamomile, can have a positive impact on your furry companion's emotional well-being, allowing him to feel calmer and more relaxed when you have to leave him alone at home. But this is just the beginning of our journey to the well-being of our adorable pets. In the second part of this chapter, we'll discover other useful resources and strategies to help your pet overcome separation anxiety. Don't miss it! In the second part of this chapter, we'll continue to explore useful resources and strategies to help your pet overcome separation anxiety. It's important to remember that every animal is unique, so it's critical to find the approach that works best for your furry companion.

In addition to using essential oils, there are other methods that can complement aromatherapy and contribute to your pet's emotional well-being. One of them is massage therapy. Through massage, you can provide your pet with a moment of relaxation and connection. Gentle, loving physical contact can reduce stress and anxiety, while strengthening the bond between the two. If you're not familiar with pet massage techniques, we recommend that you consult a professional or research books or online resources to learn the right ways to do it.

Another useful strategy to help your pet deal with separation anxiety is to establish routines and rituals. Animals feel safer and more at ease when they have a predictable daily structure. Try to set regular times to feed your pet, take them out for walks, and provide them with play and exercise time. This will help calm their anxiety and give them a sense of security knowing that they can rely on you to meet their basic needs.

In addition to daily routines, it's also important to train your pet to feel comfortable and safe when you're away. You can do this gradually, starting with short periods of separation and then gradually increasing the time. During these moments of separation, be sure to leave your pet in a pleasant and safe environment, with toys and items to keep them busy and distracted. This way, your pet will learn to associate separation with pleasant experiences instead of feeling anxious.

Socialization is also key in managing separation anxiety in pets. If possible, try to get your furry companion to have positive interactions with other animals and people. This will help strengthen your confidence and reduce any anxiety you may experience when you are alone. If your pet is struggling to socialize, you might consider working with an animal behavior trainer or therapist for guidance and support.

Finally, remember that patience and love are essential in the process of helping your pet overcome separation anxiety. Understanding that this disorder is common and treatable will give you the peace of mind you need to accompany your pet in its recovery process. If despite your best efforts, your pet's separation anxiety persists or worsens, we recommend that you see a veterinarian or animal behavior specialist for more specific evaluation and guidance.

In conclusion, separation anxiety can be challenging for both your pet and you, but there are natural and effective solutions to help alleviate it. Aromatherapy, along with other resources such as massage, routines, training and socialization, can contribute to the emotional well-being of your furry companion. Remember to adapt these strategies to your pet's individual needs and don't hesitate to seek professional help if necessary. Your pet deserves a happy, anxiety-free life!

Chapter 14:
Aromatherapy for Aging in Pets

Learn how essential oils can help pets find comfort and alleviate the symptoms of aging.

Over the course of life, our beloved furry companions also age, and it's our duty to provide them with proper care during this stage. Like humans, pets can experience a variety of symptoms related to aging, such as decreased mobility, loss of hearing and vision, joint and tissue problems, and more.

Aromatherapy, an ancient practice that uses plant-derived essential oils, can be a natural option to help alleviate some of these symptoms and provide greater well-being to our pets in their golden years. Essential oils contain bioactive compounds that can have positive effects on the body and mind, and their proper use can generate significant benefits for our beloved furry companions.

One of the main benefits of aromatherapy for aging in pets is its ability to relieve pain and inflammation in joints and tissues. As our pets age, it's common for them to experience greater stiffness and discomfort associated with diseases such as arthritis. Applying essential oils with anti-inflammatory and analgesic properties can provide natural relief and improve their mobility, allowing them to enjoy a higher quality of life.

Some essential oils recommended for relieving symptoms in joints and tissues are lavender essential oil, known for its relaxing and antispasmodic properties, as well as rosemary essential oil, renowned for its analgesic and anti-inflammatory properties. However, it is essential to consult with an expert in veterinary aromatherapy to ensure that essential oils are used safely and appropriately for each specific case.

Another important aspect of aging in pets is hearing and vision loss, which can affect their quality of life and their ability to interact with their environment. Essential oils can also help in this regard. For example, chamomile essential oil, renowned for its relaxing and anti-inflammatory properties, can help reduce eye irritation and provide relief in cases of conjunctivitis.

In addition, aromatherapy can help ease anxiety and stress associated with aging in pets. Lavender essential oil, for example, has calming properties and can promote a state of relaxation in both dogs and cats. This can be especially beneficial for those animals that may experience changes in their behavior during this stage of life.

In short, aromatherapy offers a natural and complementary alternative to help our pets find comfort and alleviate the symptoms of aging. From alleviating pain and inflammation in joints and tissues, to improving hearing and vision loss, and alleviating anxiety, essential oils can provide significant benefits for our beloved furry companions.

In the second part of this chapter, we'll further explore the application of aromatherapy in aging pets, and share specific recommendations for using essential oils safely and effectively. We'll discover how to design blends suitable for each situation and how to adapt aromatherapy to the individual needs of our pets. Don't miss it! In the second part of this chapter, we will delve into the practical application of aromatherapy in aging pets. We'll share specific recommendations and offer tips for using essential oils safely and effectively for the benefit of our beloved furry companions.

Aromatherapy for aging in pets: practical application

When it comes to using aromatherapy on our pets, it's vital to remember that every animal is unique and can react differently to essential oils. Therefore, it is essential to always consult with an expert in veterinary aromatherapy for appropriate and safe advice.

Once we have obtained the approval of a professional, we can begin using essential oils safely and for the benefit of our pets in their golden years.

One of the most common ways to apply aromatherapy to pets is by diffusing essential oils into the environment. We can use a diffuser or vaporizer specially designed for use on pets. It is important to follow the manufacturer's instructions and ensure that the device is placed in a suitable and safe place.

We can also use the direct inhalation technique. To do this, we simply add a few drops of essential oil to our hands, rub it gently and then bring our hands to our pet's snout so that it can inhale the aromas. We must be careful not to directly apply essential oils to the skin or eyes of our pets.

Another safe method of application is the dilution of essential oils in a carrier vehicle, such as vegetable oil or neutral lotion. This allows us to gently massage specific areas of our pets, such as the joints, to relieve pain and inflammation.

It is essential to remember that the quantity and concentration of essential oils used must be appropriate for each animal depending on its size, species and state of health. It is advisable to start with low concentrations and observe the reaction of our pets, gradually increasing if necessary.

We should always be on the lookout for any signs of discomfort or adverse reactions from our pets. If we notice any signs of discomfort, such as skin irritation, shortness of breath, or any other unusual symptom, we should immediately stop using essential oils and consult a veterinarian.

In addition, it is important to keep essential oils out of reach of our pets, as some of them can be toxic if ingested in large quantities. We must store them in a safe place and ensure that our pets do not have access to them.

In conclusion, aromatherapy can be a powerful tool to help our pets find comfort and alleviate the symptoms of aging. By using the right essential oils and following the recommendations of an expert in veterinary aromatherapy, we can improve the quality of life of our beloved furry companions at this stage of their lives.

Remember that it's always best to be safe and seek the guidance of trained professionals before starting any aromatherapy treatment for our pets. Through education and proper care, we can offer them greater well-being and unconditional love throughout their golden years.

Chapter 15:
Aromatherapy for Pet Training and Socialization

L earn how essential oils can be useful in the training and socialization process of your pets.

Aromatherapy is not only beneficial to humans, but it can also be a powerful tool to help our beloved pets in their training and socialization. Essential oils, extracted from plants and flowers, have therapeutic properties that can soothe, balance and stimulate our furry friends.

When it comes to pet training, patience and consistency are key. But did you know that essential oils can complement this process and help make it more effective? Through aromatherapy, we can influence the behavior and mood of our pets, making it easier for them to learn and adapt to different situations.

One of the most recommended essential oils for pet training is lavender. With its soft floral scent, lavender has a calming effect on animals, helping them to relax and concentrate on the tasks at hand. You can dilute a few drops of lavender essential oil in water and gently spray the environment during training sessions. You can also add a few drops to a cotton ball and place it near your pet so it can inhale its soothing scent.

In addition to lavender, chamomile essential oil is another ideal option for training. This oil has relaxing properties and helps relieve stress and anxiety in pets. You can mix a few drops of chamomile essential oil with water and use it as a spray to spray the area where your pet performs its training activities.

It's important to note that essential oils must be used safely and properly. Always consult a veterinarian or aromatherapy expert for specific recommendations for your pet, as some oils can be toxic to certain species. In addition, it is essential to dilute essential oils in water or another suitable vehicle before using them, as their pure concentration may be too strong for animals.

The socialization of our pets is another fundamental aspect for their emotional well-being and their integration into the community. Aromatherapy can play an important role in this process, creating a relaxing and safe environment so that our pets can interact with other animals and people in a positive way.

Orange essential oil is very useful in socializing pets. Its citrus and energizing scent promotes play and sociability. You can dilute a few drops in water and use it as a spray in areas where your pet is meeting other animals or people. Remember that every pet is unique, so it's important to observe their reactions and adjust essential oil concentrations according to their individual needs.

Through aromatherapy, we can enhance the training and socialization process of our pets, providing them with additional support to make them feel more comfortable and safer. However, it's critical to remember that aromatherapy is not a substitute for proper education and socialization. It's important to complement these techniques with positive training and the time and patience necessary for our pets to realize their full potential.

Author's note: I hope you enjoyed this first look at how aromatherapy can benefit your pets in their training and socialization! In the next part of the chapter, we'll explore more essential oils and specific techniques you can use. Don't miss it! The socialization of pets is a crucial aspect of their emotional well-being and their integration into the community. Aromatherapy can play an important role in this process, creating a relaxing and safe environment for our pets to interact positively with other animals and people.

In addition to orange essential oil, there are other options that can benefit your pets' socialization process. Vetiver essential oil, for example, is known for its calming effect on animals. This oil has an earthy, comforting scent that can help reduce anxiety and fear in social situations. You can dilute a few drops of vetiver essential oil in water and spray it gently around the area where the socialization will take place. This way, you'll create a relaxed and safe environment for your pets.

Another essential oil that can be beneficial is ylang-ylang. This oil has a sweet, floral scent that can promote trust and positive interaction between pets and other people or animals. You can add a few drops of ylang-ylang essential oil to a diffuser or spray it gently in the room during socialization sessions. This pleasant scent will help pets feel more comfortable and relaxed when interacting with others.

Remember that every pet is unique and may respond differently to essential oils. It's important to watch your reactions and adjust essential oil concentrations according to your individual needs. Some pets may be more sensitive to certain odors, so it's always a good idea to test a small amount of essential oil in a closed room and observe the reaction before using it during socialization sessions.

In addition to using essential oils, there are other socialization techniques you can incorporate into the process. Interactive play with other animals, regular outings to busy places, and gradual contact with people and other animals can help make your pets feel more comfortable and safer in different social environments.

Remember that aromatherapy is not a substitute for proper education and socialization. It's important to complement these techniques with positive training and the time and patience necessary for our pets to realize their full potential.

In short, aromatherapy can be a powerful tool for training and socializing our pets. Essential oils such as lavender, chamomile, orange, vetiver and ylang-ylang can provide additional support by creating a relaxing and safe environment. However, it's critical to remember that every pet is unique and may respond differently, so it's important to watch their reactions and adjust the concentration of essential oils as needed.

I hope these tips and techniques will be useful to you in the process of training and socializing your pets. Always remember to check with a veterinarian or aromatherapy expert for specific recommendations for your pet. Through aromatherapy and the unconditional love, we provide to our pets, we can help them live a happy and balanced life. Don't miss the next installment of this chapter, where we'll explore more essential oils and techniques specific to your pet's well-being!

Chapter 16:
Aromatherapy for energy balance in pets

Explore how essential oils can help balance your pets' energy field, promoting health and well-being.

The connection between humans and their pets is profound. Pet owners are often drawn to the balance and peace of mind that their beloved furry companions can offer them. However, just like us, our pets can also experience energy imbalances that can negatively affect their overall well-being.

This is where aromatherapy can play a significant role. Essential oils, extracted from aromatic plants, have been widely used for centuries to promote healing and balance in both humans and animals. These essences full of life have therapeutic properties that can be used to help our pets to restore their energy balance.

When considering aromatherapy for our pets, it's critical to remember that their well-being is a priority. It is essential to use essential oils with caution and always in a form suitable for use in animals. Before starting any treatment, it is important to consult an appropriate veterinarian or aromatherapy specialist who can advise us on safe oils and forms of application.

When our animals are in energy balance, their overall health improves and their mood reflects an innate joy. Essential oils can be a valuable tool to help achieve this energy balance.

One of the most commonly used essential oils in animal aromatherapy is lavender oil. This versatile and gentle oil has calming and relaxing properties that can help reduce stress and tension in our pets. By adding a few drops of lavender oil to a diffuser in the room where your pet is, you can create a calm and harmonious environment that contributes to their well-being and energy balance.

Another essential oil that is beneficial to our pets is chamomile oil. Known for its anti-inflammatory and soothing properties, this oil can be useful for relieving skin conditions or problems related to the digestive system. However, it is important to remember to properly dilute it before use and to consult with a specialist.

In addition to these oils, there are a variety of essences that can promote energy balance in our pets. Frankincense oil, for example, can be beneficial in helping to reduce anxiety and promote a state of calm. Tangerine oil, on the other hand, can help stimulate and energize pets that feel sluggish or apathetic.

In conclusion, aromatherapy offers a range of possibilities to help balance the energy field of our beloved pets. By choosing the right essential oils and using them safely, we can positively contribute to your overall well-being. Remember, however, that it's always essential to seek professional guidance before starting any essential oil treatment for your pets.

The next chapter will further explore how aromatherapy can be used in practice and the precautions we must take into account. Keep reading and discover how you can harness the power of essential oils to promote the health and happiness of your pets.

We can't wait to share the benefits and specific applications of aromatherapy for pets' energy balance. In the second half of this chapter, you'll discover how to apply essential oils safely and effectively, as well as some real success stories. Keep up the excitement, the best is yet to come! In the second half of this chapter, we're going to explore some specific ways in which we can apply aromatherapy to help balance our pets' energy field. In addition, I will share with you some real success stories that demonstrate the power of essential oils in the health and happiness of our beloved furry companions.

One of the most common ways to use aromatherapy on pets is through the topical use of essential oils. However, it is important to remember that animals have more sensitive skin than ours, so it is necessary to properly dilute the oils before applying them. You can mix a few drops of essential oil with a carrier oil such as coconut oil or sweet almond oil. This will ensure that the essential oil is distributed safely and smoothly over your pet's skin.

For example, diluted lavender essential oil can be applied as massages to help calm and relax your pet. Simply warm a few drops of diluted oil between your hands and gently massage your companion's coat. In addition to promoting a state of serenity, this massage can also provide relief from conditions such as anxiety, skin irritation or sleep problems.

Another method of topical application is through the creation of an aromatherapy spray. You can mix a few drops of essential oil with water and transfer the solution to a spray bottle. Gently spray your pet's environment or even their bed to create a relaxing and harmonious environment.

In addition to topical use, we can also use the inhalation of essential oils to balance the energy field of our pets. This can be achieved through the use of an aromatherapy diffuser. Add a few drops of essential oil to the diffuser and allow the scent to spread smoothly into the air. Not only will this help to calm and relax your pet, it can also help to eliminate unpleasant odors and purify the environment.

It's important to remember that every pet is unique and may respond differently to essential oils. That's why it's essential to always watch your pet closely after applying any essential oil. If you notice any signs of discomfort or allergic reaction, discontinue use and see a veterinarian immediately.

Now, I would like to share with you some real success stories that demonstrate the benefits of aromatherapy on the energy balance of pets. These stories show us how essential oils can make a positive difference in the lives of our pets, providing them with greater health and happiness.

Story 1: Luna, a little dog rescued from a shelter, was suffering from anxiety and stress due to her traumatic past. After consulting with an animal aromatherapy specialist, his owner began using diluted chamomile essential oil on his skin and through inhalation. Little by little, Luna began to show signs of calm and tranquility, and her anxiety decreased significantly.

Story 2: Max, an older cat with arthritis, was experiencing pain and stiffness in his joints. Its owner decided to try diluted rosemary essential oil in topical massages. After several weeks of regular application, Max began to move more easily and his quality of life improved markedly.

These stories are just two examples of how aromatherapy can be used effectively on our pets. More and more people are discovering the benefits of essential oils on the well-being of their furry companions, and as we progress through this book, we will learn more about the various applications and precautions of aromatherapy for our pets.

Remember, always consult a professional before starting any essential oil treatment on your pets and watch closely for signs of any adverse reactions. With caution and guidance, we can harness the power of aromatherapy to promote the health and happiness of our beloved pets.

Keep reading and discover everything you need to know about aromatherapy for energy balance in pets. In the next few pages, we'll explore more advanced techniques, such as acupressure and aromatherapy meditation, that can help bring your pet to a state of greater well-being. Don't miss the chance to learn more about this wonderful practice and how it can transform the lives of your pets.

Chapter 17:
Aromatherapy for Pet Disease Prevention

In our quest to keep our beloved pets healthy and happy, we often seek out different approaches and alternative therapies that can be beneficial to their well-being. Aromatherapy is an increasingly recognized practice used in humans, but did you know that it can also be a preventive measure to maintain the health of your beloved animals? In this chapter, we'll discover how aromatherapy can be used as a tool to prevent diseases in pets.

Aromatherapy has been practiced for centuries and is based on the use of essential oils extracted from aromatic plants. These oils contain powerful natural compounds that can have positive effects on the minds and bodies of animals, as well as on humans. When used properly, essential oils can help balance the immune system, strengthen the respiratory system and improve the overall health of pets.

Before you start using aromatherapy on your pets, it's important to consider some precautions. First of all, you should choose essential oils of high quality and purity, as synthetic products can be harmful to animals. In addition, pets are very sensitive to odors, so it is essential to dilute essential oils in a soft carrier, such as almond oil or jojoba, before applying them to their fur or skin. Finally, you must consider the individual needs of each pet, as some animals may be more sensitive than others.

One of the most common ways to use aromatherapy on pets is through the diffusion of essential oils into the air. This can be done using a diffuser specially designed for pets or simply by adding a few drops of essential oil to a bowl of hot water. Inhaling aromatic vapors can have a calming and relaxing effect on pets, especially during times of stress or anxiety. Some essential oils recommended for diffusion include lavender, chamomile, and vetiver.

Another way to use aromatherapy on pets is through massages and topical applications. By diluting essential oils in a suitable carrier oil, you can gently massage your pet's body, focusing on areas of tension or discomfort. In addition to providing a relaxing experience, this type of application can help strengthen the immune system and relieve muscle and joint ailments.

It's important to remember that every pet is unique and may respond differently to aromatherapy. Some animals may enjoy the smells and positive effects that essential oils can provide, while others may not feel comfortable. Always watch your pet's reactions to essential oils and consult a veterinarian specializing in aromatherapy for specific recommendations for your furry friend.

As we further explore the incredible world of aromatherapy for pets, we'll discover how this practice can be used as an effective measure of prevention and health maintenance. From strengthening the immune system to relieving stress and anxiety, aromatherapy offers a natural and encouraging approach to the comprehensive care of our adorable pets. Get ready to dive into the second half of this chapter, where we'll learn about specific essential oils and recommendations for using aromatherapy as a preventive tool in our pets' daily lives. Stay tuned and discover the true power of this ancient practice for the benefit of your faithful companions. As we continue to explore the wonderful world of aromatherapy for pets, we enter the second half of this chapter, where we will discover specific essential oils and recommendations for using aromatherapy as a preventive tool in the daily lives of our beloved pets.

One of the most popular and versatile essential oils for use in aromatherapy for pets is lavender oil. This oil has relaxing and calming properties that can help reduce stress and anxiety in pets. You can use lavender oil diluted in a carrier oil to gently massage your pet's coat or even add a few drops to their bath to create a relaxing environment.

Another essential oil that is beneficial to pets is chamomile oil. This oil is known for its anti-inflammatory properties and can be used to relieve muscle and joint ailments in pets. You can use it diluted in a carrier oil to gently massage the affected areas or even add a few drops to a diffuser in the environment where your pet spends most of its time.

Vetiver essential oil can also be used in aromatherapy for pets. This oil has calming properties and can help reduce stress and anxiety in pets, especially those that are prone to hyperactivity or have behavioral problems. You can dilute a few drops of vetiver essential oil in a carrier oil and gently massage your pet's body for a moment of relaxation.

It's important to note that not all essential oils are safe to use on pets. Some essential oils, such as tea tree oil, can be toxic to certain animals, so it is always advisable to consult a veterinarian specializing in aromatherapy before using any essential oil on your pet. Also, remember to always dilute essential oils in a suitable carrier oil and perform a sensitivity test before use.

In addition to the topical application and diffusion of essential oils, there are also other aromatherapy methods you can use to benefit your pets. For example, you can use a collar or pad impregnated with essential oils so that your pet can enjoy its benefits throughout the day. You can also add a few drops of essential oil to your bed or to a tissue you may have nearby, so you can passively enjoy the scents.

Always remember to be attentive to your pet's reactions and adjust the doses and methods of application of essential oils as needed. Every pet is unique and may respond differently to aromatherapy, so it's important to observe their behavior and consult a professional if you have any questions.

In short, aromatherapy can be an effective tool for preventing and maintaining pet health. From relaxation and stress relief to reducing muscle and joint ailments, essential oils can provide significant benefits to our beloved pets. Don't forget that getting the right advice and using high-quality and pure essential oils is key to ensuring your safety and well-being.

Thus, we conclude this chapter dedicated to aromatherapy for the prevention of diseases in pets. I hope you have enjoyed this journey because of the wonderful benefits of aromatherapy and that you can take advantage of this natural practice for the benefit of the health and well-being of your faithful companions. Always remember to give them the love, care, and attention they deserve. See you soon!

Chapter 18:
Aromatherapy for Strengthening Pet Immune Systems

Learn how to use essential oils to support and strengthen your pets' immune system.

Our beloved furry companions, our pets, are an important part of our lives. They are a constant source of love, companionship and joy. For this reason, it's crucial that we take care of their health and well-being, including their immune system.

Our pets' immune systems are responsible for protecting their bodies from disease and promoting their overall well-being. Like us, they can also face immune system disorders, making them more susceptible to infections and diseases.

Fortunately, aromatherapy can be a natural tool to strengthen and support our pets' immune systems. Essential oils, derived from plants and flowers, have therapeutic properties that can help boost your bodies' natural defenses.

The proper use of essential oils can offer a variety of benefits for your pets' immune system. Some essential oils, such as lavender essential oil, have antibacterial and antiviral properties that can help prevent infections and strengthen your immune system.

In addition, certain essential oils, such as tea tree essential oil, have anti-inflammatory properties that can reduce inflammation and promote a healthy immune response.

However, before you start using essential oils on your pets, it's important to consult a veterinarian or aromatherapy specialist to make sure you're using the right oils and in the right doses. Not all essential oils are safe for all pets, and some can be toxic if used improperly.

Once you've consulted a professional, there are several ways to use essential oils to strengthen your pets' immune systems. One option is to diffuse the oils into the air using a special diffuser for pets. This will allow them to inhale the therapeutic benefits of the oils and strengthen their immune system naturally.

Another option is to apply the oils directly to your pets' skin. However, it is crucial to properly dilute oils in a carrier oil before applying them, as they are highly concentrated and can be irritating if used undiluted.

Also, remember to pay attention to your pet's reaction to essential oils. Some pets may be sensitive to certain oils, so it's important to watch for any signs of discomfort or irritation and to stop using the oil if necessary.

In short, aromatherapy can be a powerful tool for strengthening your pets' immune system. The right essential oils, used with caution and in the right doses, can offer therapeutic benefits and promote the health and well-being of your dear furry friends.

By continuing to explore the beneficial properties of essential oils for our pets, you'll discover even more ways to support their immune systems and keep them healthy and happy. In the second half of this chapter, we'll reveal some additional essential oils and how you can incorporate them into your animal care routine. Stay tuned and keep learning about this fascinating natural therapy!

In the second half of this chapter, we'll explore some additional essential oils that may be beneficial to your pets' immune systems and how you can incorporate them into their care routine. Remember to always take precautions when using essential oils and consult a veterinarian or aromatherapy specialist to make sure you're using the right oils and in the right doses.

One of the most popular and versatile essential oils is lemon essential oil. This citrus oil has antibacterial and antiviral properties, making it an excellent option for strengthening your pets' immune system. You can add a few drops of lemon essential oil to a diffuser or dilute it in a carrier oil to apply it topically. You can also use it to clean your living spaces, as the refreshing smell of lemon will help to purify the environment.

Another essential oil that can be beneficial is eucalyptus essential oil. This oil has antimicrobial and anti-inflammatory properties, which can help prevent diseases and strengthen your pets' immune systems. However, it is important to note that eucalyptus is not safe for all pets, especially for cats and dogs of sensitive breeds such as greyhounds or whippets. Before using eucalyptus essential oil, be sure to consult a veterinarian.

Chamomile essential oil is another great ally to strengthen your pets' immune system. Known for its anti-inflammatory and soothing properties, chamomile can help reduce stress and promote a healthy immune response in your pets. You can diffuse a few drops of chamomile essential oil into the air or dilute it in a carrier oil to gently massage your pets, especially if they suffer from anxiety or skin problems.

Last but not least, ginger essential oil can also be beneficial to your immune system. Ginger has anti-inflammatory and antioxidant properties, which can help strengthen the immune system and reduce inflammation in your pets' bodies. You can use ginger essential oil in a diffuser or dilute it in a carrier oil to massage your pets.

Remember that every pet is unique and they may have different reactions to essential oils. It is important to pay attention to any signs of discomfort or irritation and to adjust the dose or discontinue use if necessary. In addition, always dilute essential oils in a carrier oil before applying them topically to avoid possible irritation to your skin.

In short, aromatherapy can be a natural and effective tool for strengthening your pets' immune system. The right essential oils, used with caution and in the right doses, can offer therapeutic benefits and promote the health and well-being of your dear furry friends. From lavender essential oil to ginger essential oil, exploring and experimenting with the benefits of aromatherapy will allow you to find the best options for strengthening your pets' immune systems.

As you continue to learn about this fascinating natural therapy, you'll be equipped with additional tools to support your pets' well-being. Always remember the importance of consulting a veterinarian or aromatherapy specialist before using essential oils and keep discovering how you can provide the best care and affection to your beloved furry companions.

Keep exploring and taking advantage of the benefits of aromatherapy for strengthening your pets' immune systems!

Chapter 19:
Aromatherapy as an Adjunct to Veterinary Medicine

Explore how aromatherapy can complement traditional veterinary treatments to improve the health and well-being of pets.

In today's world, veterinary medicine has advanced significantly, providing our beloved pets with a better quality of life and greater opportunities for care. However, as we discover new alternatives to promote animal welfare, we come across the fascinating practice of aromatherapy. This ancient technique, used for centuries on human beings, has now become a promising option to support the health of our faithful companions.

Aromatherapy is based on the use of essential oils extracted from different plants and flowers. These oils have therapeutic properties and can be used in a variety of ways, such as massages, inhalations or diffusers. Through their scent, essential oils have the ability to influence our mood, alleviate physical ailments and promote relaxation. Now, thanks to scientific studies and testimonials from pet owners, we know that they can also be beneficial for our furry friends.

When we talk about aromatherapy applied to pets, it is important to highlight the importance of the safety and quality of the essential oils used. Not all oils are suitable for our pets and some can be harmful or toxic to them. It is essential to get information and purchase essential oils from reliable and certified suppliers. In addition, essential oil must always be diluted before application, as animal skin is more sensitive than human skin.

One of the most prominent benefits of aromatherapy in animals is its ability to relieve stress and anxiety. Just like people, our pets can also experience negative emotions that affect their overall well-being. Essential oils, such as lavender or chamomile, can be used to create a relaxing environment at home or to relieve stress during stressful situations, such as visits to the vet or traveling.

In addition, aromatherapy can become a valuable complement to the treatment of specific health problems. Some essential oils have antibacterial or anti-inflammatory properties that can help relieve certain ailments. For example, tea tree essential oil has been used successfully in treating canine ear infections, while peppermint may be useful for relieving muscle aches in more active pets.

It is important to note that aromatherapy is not intended to replace, but to complement, traditional veterinary care. You should always consult your veterinarian before using any complementary technique on your pets, as each animal is unique and may respond differently to treatments. Your veterinarian will best guide you in choosing the right products and the safe ways to use aromatherapy.

In short, aromatherapy has proven to be a valuable option for the well-being of our pets. From relieving stress and anxiety to providing support in treating certain ailments, essential oils can be a beneficial addition to the lives of our furry friends. However, safety and veterinary advice are key to ensuring positive outcomes. In the second half of this chapter, we'll explore practical examples of how aromatherapy has been successfully used in pet care. Don't miss it! In the second half of this chapter, we'll explore practical examples of how aromatherapy has been successfully used in pet care. These examples will inspire you and give you ideas on how to implement aromatherapy into the daily lives of your beloved furry companions.

One of the most prominent benefits of aromatherapy for pets is its ability to promote relaxation during stressful situations. For example, if your dog gets nervous during car trips, you can use essential oils such as chamomile or lavender to create a relaxing environment in the vehicle. Simply add a few drops of oil to a diffuser or tissue and place it in your pet's rest area. The soft, soothing scent will help your dog stay calm during the trip.

In addition, aromatherapy can also be beneficial in relieving physical aches and pains in pets. For example, if your cat suffers from arthritis, you can use essential oils such as ginger or rosemary, which have anti-inflammatory properties, to relieve inflammation and reduce pain. Dilute a few drops of the oil in a base oil such as coconut oil and gently massage the affected area. This can provide relief and improve your cat's mobility.

Another useful application of aromatherapy is in the treatment of skin problems in pets. Some essential oils, such as tea tree or lavender, have antibacterial and antifungal properties that can help fight infections and promote healthy skin. To treat skin problems in your pet, dilute the essential oil in a base oil and apply it directly to the affected area. Always remember to check with your veterinarian before using any treatment on your pet.

It's important to mention that aromatherapy can be adapted to the individual needs of each pet. For example, if your dog has anxiety problems in specific situations, such as during storms or fireworks, you can create a personalized blend of essential oils that are more effective for him. Remember that every pet is unique and may respond differently to treatments, so it's essential to experiment and see how your pet reacts to different essential oils.

In addition to the therapeutic benefits, aromatherapy can also help strengthen the bond between you and your pet. By using aromatherapy in your daily care, you're creating a calm and relaxing environment that promotes confidence and well-being. Both you and your pet can enjoy the benefits of aromatherapy together, creating moments of relaxation and connection.

Remember, you should always consult your veterinarian before using any complementary techniques on your pets. They can provide guidance specific to your pet's individual needs and ensure that you're using safe, quality essential oils.

In conclusion, aromatherapy can be a valuable complement to traditional veterinary medicine to improve the health and well-being of our pets. From relieving stress and anxiety to treating physical ailments, essential oils can be a powerful tool in caring for our beloved pets. Always remember to follow safety guidelines and consult your veterinarian to ensure positive results. Take care of your pet naturally and provide them with the well-being they deserve!

Chapter 20:
Aromatherapy Recipes for Caring for Your Pet

Aromatherapy is a great way to promote the well-being of our pets naturally. Essential oils, extracted from plants and flowers, have therapeutic properties that can help alleviate different ailments and promote a sense of calm and balance in our beloved furry companions.

In this chapter, we're going to share with you a variety of recipes and essential oil blends that you can use in your pet's daily care. These blends have been carefully selected and tested to ensure their effectiveness and safety.

Before you start using aromatherapy on your pet, it's important to consider some precautions. First, you should always consult your veterinarian before using any essential oil. Every pet is unique and their health may be sensitive to certain components. In addition, it is essential to use quality essential oils and to dilute them properly before applying them to your pet.

One of the most popular recipes for relaxing your pet is a mixture of lavender and chamomile. These two essential oils have calming properties and can be especially useful in times of stress or anxiety. To prepare this mixture, dilute 2 drops of lavender essential oil and 2 drops of chamomile essential oil in 30 ml of a carrier oil such as sweet almond oil. Then, gently massage this mixture into your pet's coat or add it to an aromatherapy diffuser in the room where your pet spends most of its time.

If your pet has skin problems, such as itching or irritation, a mixture of tea tree essential oil and coconut oil can be very beneficial. Tea tree oil has antimicrobial and anti-inflammatory properties, while coconut oil moisturizes and soothes the skin. Mix 2 drops of tea tree essential oil and 1 tablespoon of coconut oil in a bowl. Then, apply this mixture to the affected areas of your pet's skin and massage gently.

To combat fleas and ticks naturally, you can use a mixture of eucalyptus essential oil and neem oil. These two essential oils have repellent properties and can help keep unwanted insects at bay. Dilute 2 drops of eucalyptus essential oil and 2 drops of neem oil in 30 ml of distilled water. Then spray this mixture on your pet's fur, avoiding contact with the eyes and mouth.

Remember that every pet is unique and may respond differently to essential oils. It's important to watch your pet during and after using aromatherapy, and to watch for any adverse reactions. If you notice any signs of discomfort or irritation, stop using essential oils and consult your veterinarian.

We'll continue to explore more aromatherapy recipes and blends for caring for your pet in the second part of this chapter. Are you ready to discover new ways to improve the health and well-being of your furry companion? Stay tuned and keep reading to find more aromatic surprises! In the second half of this chapter, we want to continue sharing with you recipes and aromatherapy blends for caring for your pet. These combinations have been designed to address different needs and promote a healthy and balanced environment for your beloved furry companion.

If your pet has digestion problems, a mixture of peppermint and ginger essential oil can go a long way. Peppermint is known for its digestive properties, and ginger can help relieve nausea and indigestion. To prepare this mixture, dilute 2 drops of peppermint essential oil and 2 drops of ginger essential oil in 30 ml of a carrier oil such as jojoba oil. Gently apply this mixture to the skin of your pet's abdomen and massage clockwise for a few minutes. You can also add a few drops of this mixture to your food to boost its benefits.

If your pet is suffering from stress or anxiety while traveling, a lavender and tangerine essential oil blend can go a long way. Lavender provides a sense of calm and relaxation, while mandarin has a calming effect and can help relieve tension. To prepare this mixture, dilute 2 drops of lavender essential oil and 2 drops of mandarin essential oil in 30 ml of a carrier oil such as coconut oil. Gently apply this mixture to your pet's coat before a trip or place a few drops on their collar or bed so they can inhale the relaxing scents along the way.

If your pet is suffering from insect bites or skin irritation, a blend of lavender and chamomile essential oil can provide relief and promote healing. Both essential oils have anti-inflammatory and soothing properties that can reduce swelling and itching. To prepare this mixture, dilute 2 drops of lavender essential oil and 2 drops of chamomile essential oil in 30 ml of olive oil. Apply this mixture gently to the affected areas of your pet's skin and massage carefully. You'll notice that the irritation decreases and your pet will feel more comfortable.

Another useful mix for caring for your pet is a combination of cedar and lemon essential oil to naturally repel fleas and ticks. These two essential oils have repellent properties and can help keep unwanted insects at bay. To prepare this mixture, dilute 2 drops of cedar essential oil and 2 drops of lemon essential oil in 30 ml of distilled water. Then, gently spray this mixture onto your pet's coat, avoiding contact with the eyes and mouth. In addition to repelling fleas and ticks, this mixture will leave a fresh and pleasant scent on your pet.

Remember that every pet is unique and may respond differently to essential oils. It's important to watch your pet during and after using aromatherapy, and to watch for any adverse reactions. Always use quality essential oils and dilute them properly before applying them to your pet. If in doubt or if your pet shows a negative reaction, consult your veterinarian.

We hope that these aromatherapy recipes and blends will help you improve the health and well-being of your furry companion. Take care of your pet naturally and strengthen your bond through the benefits of aromatherapy. Keep exploring and experimenting with the different mixes to find the ones that best suit your pet's needs.

Remember, there are always more aromatic surprises to discover on the path to the well-being of your pets! Keep reading and learning about aromatherapy to continue providing them with the care they deserve.

Disclaimer

The information provided in this book is for general informational and educational purposes only and is not intended as a substitute for professional advice, diagnosis, or treatment. The author and publisher have made every effort to ensure the accuracy and reliability of the information provided within these pages, but they make no guarantees, either express or implied, regarding the content's completeness, accuracy, or applicability.

Neither the author nor the publisher shall be held liable or responsible for any misunderstanding or misuse of the information contained in this book or for any loss, damage, or injury caused, or alleged to be caused, directly or indirectly by any treatment, action, or application of any advice discussed in this publication. The statements made within this book are not intended to diagnose, treat, cure, or prevent any disease. Readers should consult with a qualified healthcare provider for medical advice tailored to their personal circumstances.

The views and opinions expressed herein are those of the author alone and do not necessarily reflect the official policy or position of any agency or company. All content provided in this book is on an "as-is" basis and the author and publisher disclaim all responsibility for any errors or omissions.

Don't miss out!

Visit the website below and you can sign up to receive emails whenever Gonzalo Estrada publishes a new book. There's no charge and no obligation.

https://books2read.com/r/B-A-OZBBB-JDFZC

BOOKS2READ

Connecting independent readers to independent writers.

Also by Gonzalo Estrada

Self Healing
Visualiza tu Éxito
Cultivando Líderes
Afirmaciones y Empoderamiento
Semillas de Cambio
Cómo convertir TikTok en una máquina de hacer dinero
Cómo hacer dinero con Pinterest
Cómo hacer un ensayo
Cómo Pedir un Aumento de Sueldo
Currículo Poderoso
Entrenamiento sin Violencia
Entrevista Laboral
Gana Dinero con X (Twitter)
Ganar Masa Muscular
Volver a Empezar; el arte de reinventarse
Analiza Resuelve Ejecuta
Aromatherapy, The natural path to your pet´s well being
Holistic Feeding
The ABC of educating your Pet
The Art of Cosmic Connection
The Art of Feng Shui applied to your Pets